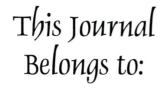

# This Journal Belongs to:

_____

_____

_____

"As most gardeners will testify, the desire to make a garden is often followed by a desire to write down your experiences there in a notebook, or a letter to a friend who gardens..."

- Michael Pollan

"or like me to draw and paint your observations."

- Mary Selinski

Thistledown
Studio

## Thistledown Studio

# How to use this Journal:

- Illustrations are representative of seasons inside and outside of my home & garden.

- To keep a garden journal i.e. weather conditions, arrival of birds, butterflies, frost date, snow from the window sills that catch the winter sun to forcing bulbs and twigs to speed up the blooming time and bring color and fragrance to dull winter days.

## Acknowledgements: A heartfelt thanks goes to graphic artist, Loretta Prindle for layout, design and friendship. I also want to thank Kim Jones at PSC Digital for all the photographic services over the past number of years.

## Statement: This project is partially supported by City Arts Funds from the Springfield Area Arts Council and the City of Springfield.

Publisher: Thistledown Studio
6309 Brent Avenue
Springfield, Illinois 62712

Cover: "Paperwhites"

# Personal Notes

# Birthdays & Anniversaries

# Important Dates

# January

## Dates of Importance

Martin Luther King - third Monday

**1** New Year's Day

**2**

**3**

**4**

**5**

**6**

**7**

" The lesson I have thoroughly learned, and wish to pass on to others, is to know the enduring happiness that the love of a garden brings."

Anonymous

Cyclamin

African Violet

# January

**8**

**9**

**10**

**11**

**12**

**13**

**14**

# January

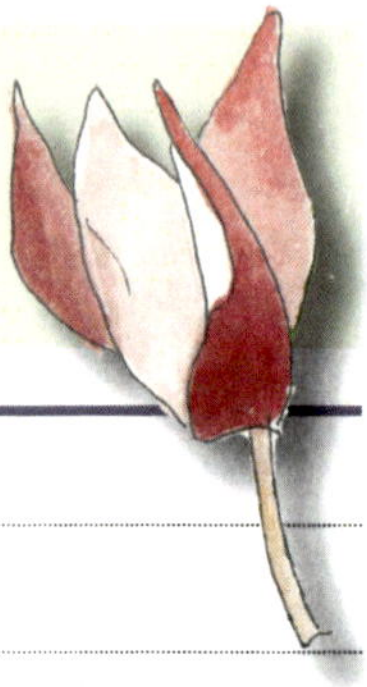

**15**

**16**

**17**

**18**

**19**

**20**

**21**

"January Poinsettia"

# January

**22**

**23**

**24**

**25**

**26**

**27**

**28**

# January

## 29

## 30

## 31

## Garden Notes

Don't forget the birds – Black sunflower seeds (oil seeds) are higher in oil content. These fatty seeds are perfect for helping birds get a burst of high energy during the winter and are less expensive.

## Think Natural

Try using Vitamin E oils, or aloe vera for your hands and legs. Lavender oil is one of the best moisturizing oils. You can dilute this oil in your regular moisturizers and use it.

# Cymbidium

"Life begins the day you start a garden."

–Chinese proverb

# February

February 29 - Leap Year

**1**

**2** Groundhog Day

**3**

**4**

**5**

**6**

**7**

# February

**8**

**9**

**10**

**11**

**12** Lincoln's Birthday

**13**

**14** Valentine's Day

# Casa Blanca Lily

"Art, to me, is the interpretation of the impression which nature makes upon the eye and the brain."

–Childe Hassam

Hydrangeas

# February

**15**

**16**

**17**

**18**

**19**

**20**

**21**

# February

**22**

**23**

**24**

**25**

**26**

**27**

**28**

MBelinski

"Too Pretty to Eat"

"First of the Season"

# February

## Notes

<br><br><br><br><br><br><br><br><br><br>

## Garden Notes

Cut back and/or prune hydrangeas and clematis according to the type of variety. 'Anna' hydrangeas bloom bigger on new wood.

Try forcing: honeysuckle, apple blossom or lilac or pussy willow this month.

# March

## Dates of Importance

Ides of March - Vernal Equinox

**1**

**2**

**3**

**4**

**5**

**6**

**7**

# Pansy

"Is any moment of the year more delightful than the present? What there is wanting in glow of colour is more than made up for in fullness of interest. Each day some well-known, long-remembered plant bursts into blossom."

– Henry A. Bright
*A year in a Lancashire Garden 1879*

# Muscari *armeniacum*

"If apple blooms in March, for fruit you may search."

– Anonymous

# March

**8**

**9**

**10**

**11**

**12**

**13**

**14**

# March

**15**

**16**

**17** St. Patrick's Day

**18**

**19**

**20** First day of Spring

**21**

*Oxalis*

# Wood Violets

M. Belinski

"Rain in the Spring is as precious as oil."

– Chinese proverb

# March

**22**

**23**

**24**

**25**

**26**

**27**

**28**

# March

## 29

## 30

## 31

## Notes

---

## Garden Notes

Sow or plant outdoors: onions, peas, potatoes, radishes, spinach, turnip and beets 5-6 weeks before last frost (mid April).

Don't walk in your garden until the soil is dry because you compact the soil. Be sure tools are clean and sharp.

LAWN: Be sure to prepare for spring fertilizer and complete before Mother's Day in May.

"The longer I live the more beautiful life becomes. If you foolishly ignore beauty, you will soon find yourself without it. Your life will be impoverished. But if you invest in beauty, it will remain with you all the days of your life."

– Frank Lloyd Wright

## Portulaca 'Moss Rose'

# April

Mid-April - Average date of Last Frost

**1**    April Fool's Day

**2**

**3**

**4**

**5**

**6**

**7**

# April

8

9

10

11

12

13

14

# Violets and Lily of the Valley

Pansies

# April

**15**

**16**

**17**

**18**

**19**

**20**

**21**

# April

**22**

**23**

**24**

**25**

**26**

**27**

**28**

"I wandered lonely as a Cloud that floats on high o'er vales and hills, when all at once I saw a crowd, a host, of golden Daffodils; beside the lake, beneath the trees, fluttering and dancing in the breeze."

– "I Wandered Lonely as a Cloud"
by William Wordsworth, 1st verse only of the four

Purple Saucer Magnolia

# April

## 29

## 30

## Notes

## Garden Notes

Prune deadwood in roses - apply early fertilizer. I like to use a 5 gallon bucket of water with 3/4 c of Epsom salts diluted on rose bush and lilac bush once a year in the Spring.

Start a plant list as you purchase new annuals and perennials.

# May

Second Sunday – Mother's Day
Fourth Monday – Memorial Day

**1**

**2**

**3**

**4**

**5** Cinco de Mayo

**6**

**7**

# "White Ruffles"

"Man has availed himself of the great laws of evolution in mightier matters than the Iris, but in no theatre of his unsleeping efforts has he created purer beauty or wakened for flower lovers a truer joy than among the bearded Irises of June."

– Eden Phillpotts in Country Life Magazine 1917

# Clematis 'Jackmanii'

"Early to bed. Early to rise.
Work like hell and fertilize."
— Emily Whaley

# May

## 8

## 9

## 10

## 11

## 12

## 13

## 14

# May

## 15

## 16

## 17

## 18

## 19

## 20

## 21

# Dogwood

# May

**22**

**23**

**24**

**25**

**26**

**27**

**28**

# May

## 29

## 30

## 31

### Notes

### Garden Notes

Plant garlic and parsley next to roses. Friend's advice: put a banana peel in hole for delphiniums; put orange peels in hole for roses.

LAWN CARE: Spring fertilize before Mother's Day

# Hydrangeas

"The rose doth deserve the chiefest place amongst all flowers whatsoever; being not only esteemed for its beauty, virtues and fragrant and odoriferous smell but also because it is the honor and ornament of our English Scepter."

– John Gerard 1597

"Pete's Roses"

# June

Third Sunday – Father's Day

**1**

**2**

**3**

**4**

**5**

**6**

**7**

# June

**8**

**9**

**10**

**11**

**12**

**13**

**14** June 14 – Flag Day

"Black and White"

# June

## 15

## 16

## 17

## 18

## 19

## 20

## 21
First day of Summer

# June

**22**

**23**

**24**

**25**

**26**

**27**

**28**

# Hydrangeas

# June

## 29

## 30

## Notes

## Garden Notes

Keep lawn trimmed to 2 $\frac{1}{2}$" as it is usually the peak growing season for cool weather grass.

Fertilize roses once each month until September.

# July

**1**

**2**

**3**

**4** Independence Day

**5**

**6**

**7**

# Queen Anne's Lace

"Dog Days of Summer is used to describe an exceedingly hot spell, usually in August. It can be traced to the early Egyptians, who held the theory that the appearance of Sirus, the dog star, rising with the sun added to its heat. The Dog Days run from about July 3-August 11."

— Eileen Mears, *State Journal Register 7/24/91*

# July

**8**

**9**

**10**

**11**

**12**

**13**

**14**

# July

**15**

**16**

**17**

**18**

**19**

**20**

**21**

# Peppers

# July

**22**

**23**

**24**

**25**

**26**

**27**

**28**

# July

## 29

## 30

## 31

## Notes

## Garden Notes

Keep flowers dead-headed for repeat blooms.

Prune Spring flowering bushes such as; forsythia, dwarf lilac, mock orange, etc.

Harvest 1st crop of lavender July 4th.

Geraniums

## "Postcards From the Beach"

# August

## Dates of Importance

State Fair Time

1

2

3

4

5

6

7

# August

**8**

**9**

**10**

**11**

**12**

**13**

**14**

"Sanchris Waterlily"

"Study nature, love nature, stay close to nature. It will never fail you."

– Frank Lloyd Wright

"A *flower* is an educated weed."
– Luther Burbank

"Asian Lilies"

# August

**15**

**16**

**17**

**18**

**19**

**20**

**21**

# August

**22**

**23**

**24**

**25**

**26**

**27**

**28**

# Hollyhocks

"The Bradfords are Coming"

M Selinski

"Everything is good in its season."

– Italian proverb

# August

## 29

## 30

## 31

## Notes

## Garden Notes

# September

## Dates of Importance

Labor Day - 1st Monday
Grandparent's Day - 1st Sunday

**1**

**2**

**3**

**4**

**5**

**6**

**7**

"Good Morning Sunshine"

"He who shares the joy of what has grown,
spreads joy abroad and doubles his own."
– Anonymous

# "Cauliflower"

# September

8

9

10

11

12

13

14

# September

**15**

**16**

**17**

**18**

**19**

**20**

**21**

M. SELINSKI

# September

**22**

**23** First day of Autumn

**24**

**25**

**26**

**27**

**28**

# September

## 29

## 30

## Notes

 ## Garden Notes

Plan to apply fall fertilizer to your lawn after Labor Day.

Bring house plants indoor but spray with insecticide first. Dry out

Amaryllis - cut leaves off the base of bulbs and store in Vermiculite.

Keep cool & dry. Order tulip/spring bulbs. Dig up old non-productive

bulbs and discard. Fertilize bed with 5-10-5.

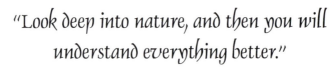

"Look deep into nature, and then you will understand everything better."

– Albert Einstein

# October

## Dates of Importance

Columbus Day - 2nd Monday
1st frost date mid October

1

2

3

4

5

6

7

# October

8

9

10

11

12

13

14

"Pumpkin Patch"

"Applebarn Pumpkins"

# October

**15**

**16**

**17**

**18**

**19**

**20**

**21**

# October

**22**

**23**

**24**

**25**

**26**

**27**

**28**

"Peek-a-Boo"

"Molly Cat"

# October

**29**

**30**

**31**  Halloween

## Notes

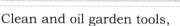
**Garden Notes**

Clean and oil garden tools,

Wrap/cover lawn furniture,

Bring in all clay pots to prevent breakage,

# November

## Dates of Importance

Election Day - 1st Tuesday
Thanksgiving - last Thursday

**1**

**2**

**3**

**4**

**5**

**6**

**7**

"Autumn Leaves"

"Maple Leaves"

# November

**8**

**9**

**10**

**11** Veteran's Day

**12**

**13**

**14**

# November

**15**

**16**

**17**

**18**

**19**

**20**

**21**

"End of Summer"

"No fruit, no flower,
no leaves, no birds
—November."

– Old English Saying

"Carving Lesson"

# November

22

23

24

25

26

27

28

# November

## 29

## 30

## Notes

 **Garden Notes**

"Washington Park, Christmas"

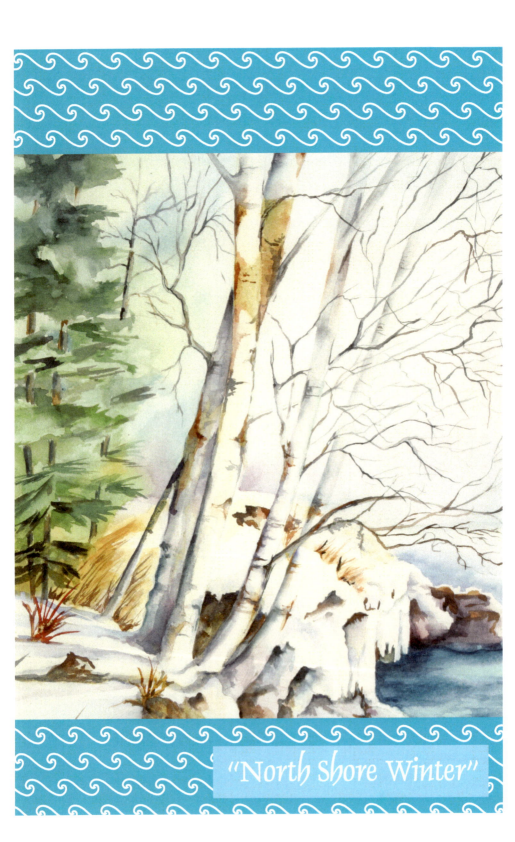

"North Shore Winter"

# December

## Dates of Importance

**1**

**2**

**3**

**4**

**5**

**6**

**7** Pearl Harbor

# December

8

9

10

11

12

13

14

*"Spontaneous"*

"Pine Cone Sketch"

# December

**15**

**16**

**17**

**18**

**19**

**20**

**21** First Day of Winter

# December

**22**

**23**

**24**

Christmas Day

**25**

**26**

**27**

**28**

"For Unto Us A Child is Given" - Handel

# December

**29**

**30**

**31** Official end of WWII, New Year's Eve

## Notes

## Garden Notes

Watch for new garden catalogues.

# Saint Fiacre

A ugust 30th is the feast day of Saint Fiacre. He is recognized as the patron saint of gardeners since the Middle Ages.

He was raised in a monastery in Ireland and much later lived in France. He fed the hungry and healed the sick with herbs from his garden and prayed for all who came to him.

Even after his death around 670 A.D. people continued to visit the monastery and as legend notes, received spiritual and physical healing.

For more detailed information: http://county.milwaukee.gov/StFiacre10506.htm